RAINBOWS LIVE AT EASTER

Library of Congress Catalog Number: 74-83413
ISBN—0-914850-07-5

RAINBOWS LIVE AT EASTER

Gloria Gaither

Photography by Bill Grine

impact
books

Also by Gloria Gaither
MAKE WARM NOISES
(MO492)

Foreword

There is a poem by Sara Teasdale that I used to teach in high school literature called "Life Has Loveliness to Sell." I like that. Loveliness isn't always free, but it is always available. Often it has to be dug out or searched for—sometimes it comes as the result of a large investment of just plain old hard work, sweat and tears. Often it happens to you like a rainbow after the storm. But life always offers its priceless rewards if we're willing to pay, to work, to *notice* mostly—in short, to invest something in life.

The rainbows—the lovelinesses—have come to me from different sources: from children, from humanity and just plain living, from daring to learn to love. I'd like to share some of the rainbows life has wrapped around my world in the hopes that you will take the risk of investing something in life and maybe stumble over a few rainbows of your own.

Table of Contents

5   Foreword

Part One   **9**   **Rainbows Come With Children**

13   What's It All About . . .?
14   Good News And Bad News
16   Hey There, In Your Underwear
18   The Risk
20   Prints
22   Grandmas Are For Sharing The Moon
25   Raw Material
26   More Than Air
29   The Game
31   Perspective
34   No Looking Back
36   Rainbows Live At Easter
39   To Be A Man
41   Children
43   Value
44   Tomorrow

Part Two   **47**   **Rainbows In The Mainstream**

51   Sunday Is For That
52   Reinforcement
55   Wish I Could
56   This Day
59   A Regular Day
60   Home
63   This House
64   "Until A Year From June Do Us Part . . ."
66   The Tiny Soap That Grew
70   Life's School
73   Compassion
74   The Real Thing

Part Three   **77**   **Rainbows And Love**

80   Eden
83   The Fighter
85   Il Fait Froid, Mon Coeur
86   Friendship
88   Worth The Risk
89   Upward Mobility
90   Until I See You
92   To Sing Is The Thing
95   Ode To Autumn
97   I Like Being Married To You

PART
1

Rainbows Come With Children

What's It All About...?

You were so excited on that first Sunday after your third birthday. You would finally graduate from the nursery (baby-land, uck!) to that grown-up place called "Class." Class sounded like school to you and school meant *big* like sister. Three-year-olds were allowed to go to "class". Even the way you said the word had a sort of sophisticated ring to it.

You were hardly out of bed that morning before you rounded up your purse, your nickles, *they take an offering in class,* and a couple of books, *everyone knows you need books for class*. These you carried to the breakfast table and the bathtub.

Finally ready with your lacy dress and your pert pink ribbons in your hair, you skipped to the door so anxious to get to "class." Then you stopped, turned a suddenly serious little face back toward us and asked, "But will that teacher really love Amy?"

In our hearts we wanted to race to you, scoop you up in our arms, assure you, protect you, shower you with life-time guaran-tees. Or better yet, we longed to spin once more the cocoon of our womb tightly around you and stop the clock on this very special three-year-old day. But inside we also knew that you had to reach and stretch and risk and learn. You had to *live*. And so we said, "Of course she will! Now run along. We'll be right there when class is over."

As the door closed behind you leaving more than the hush of your silence, but the vacuum of your absence as well, I was overwhelmed by the wisdom of your questions once again.

You *knew* the building with its late-model architecture and up-to-the-minute decor. You were familiar with the well-equipped room, sparkling clean and inviting in the morning sun, filled with happy eye-level pictures and creative playthings. But you zeroed in on the real issue—as you always seem to do.

Love—we couldn't vote that in or requisition it or donate extra allotments for future use. Love—that doesn't come from supply houses or paint cans or carpet stores. But that illusive ingredient—you said it—was the only thing that really mattered after all. And the forever impression of "God's House" you were about to get was in someone else's hands.

So we breathed a prayer for you—and for them—and began what was to become a life-long habit of trusting you to Jesus.

Good News and Bad News

"How was your day at school?"
        I asked as you sat in the tub
        soaking off the day's collection
        of grime and odors.
                "Okay, I guess."
"Oh, c'mon. What happened?"
                "Well, good things and bad.
                You know I told you I couldn't
                seem to get everyone to be friends
                at the same time?
                Well, Sally and Susan both like
                me okay, but they wouldn't
                play with each other.
                But today I got them to make up
                and be friends."

"That's great. Don't you think?"
"Well, yes, but they both got to
playing together so well
that they left me out
and I was alone the rest of the day."
"Oh . . ."
I waited in silence.
And you shrugged your little
boney, soapy shoulders
and looked at me timidly.
"Oh, well.
Blessed are peacemakers."
Then you managed a crooked little grin
that made me know
that today was being chalked up
to your store of wisdom,
and that the growing you had done
would somehow make tomorrow
a little bit richer for it.

Hey There,
In Your Underwear

When I found you, you were standing on the seventh step
　　huddled up close to the wall,
　　　　looking very small in just your underwear.
　　　　　　("Benjy's standard uniform" we call it and grin.)
　　　　But you weren't grinning
　　　　　　your tiny face was very serious—
　　　　　　　　almost stricken—
　　　　　　and there was "I can't cope, Mom" in your eyes
　　　　　　　　and there was pleading in your tone.
　　"Look!" you confided,
　　　　　　　　"I'm getting little!
　　　　　　　　　I can't, I'm getting little!"
The excitement of an hour ago was gone.
The cheers of "Oh, boy! A party with lots of kids"
　　　　　　had vanished when the doorbell rang.
　　　　'Cause there they were, no longer fantasies—real kids.
　　　　And you suddenly knew you were the littlest one,
　　　　　　and not "mama's big boy" anymore.
So when I said, "Benjy, answer the door," you ran—
　　　　the other way.
And here you are.
Trying to tell me that you feel yourself shrinking
　　　　　　in the face of real life,
　　　　　　　　real people putting your maturity on the line.
How,
when you are only three,
　　can I touch you,
　　　　or tell you,
　　　　　　that I know what you're feeling?
　　　　　　　　You there, in your underwear.

16

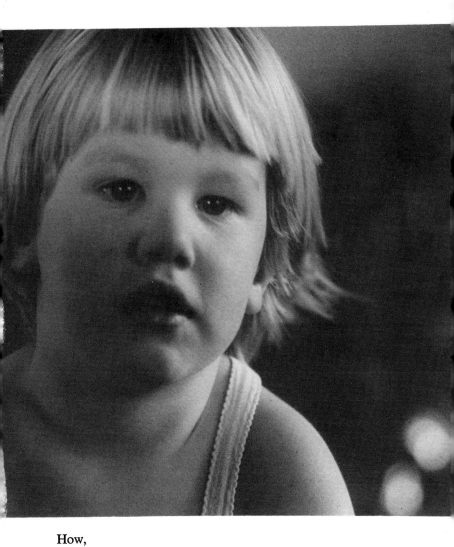

How,
in the way I hold you close,
can I let you know that I feel like running,
find myself shrinking,
and know I'm inadequate sometimes.
And how can I help you know that someday,
when you can no longer fit in my arms
or reach for Daddy's hand
and thus grow brave enough to face the onslaught of most
anything—that there is One
whose hand and whose arms you can't outgrow.

The Risk

He started to sock her right in the nose
when she took it away from him.
His lip was pouted out,
his eyes were flashing,
his tiny little fist was clinched tight
and drawn back to let her have it!
Then something magic happened.
His tiny fist stopped in mid-air
as his eyes met the eyes of his gentle little sister,
waiting for the blow to find its mark.

His face softened,
the pout disappeared,
his eyes lost their fire,
and his tiny ardent fist turned to gentle hands
that threw themselves around her little neck.
He laid his head against her cheek tenderly
and said something that sounded like
"Ahh-sister!"

It isn't worth it, I thought.
It isn't worth it to get even
to make sure she gets what's coming to her,
to settle the score.
When you win, you lose.
Oh, you may win the battle,
but you always lose the war.

A dozen larger battlefields paraded themselves through my mind.
Times when I could have loved longer
but I had had to be "right" instead.
Times when I could have gone the second mile
but I was too elated about being first to the finish line.
Times when I won, but lost.

Love is always a risk.
Love leaves you open to attack.
Love makes you vulnerable,
you get hurt.
But to make the fatal choice to be safe
is to choose to be dead.

So sometimes you lose,
only to find that in reality you've won.

Isn't that better than winning to lose?

I'd come to the playroom to referee a battle.
But instead I stood in awe of love's transforming embrace.

19

Prints

I hope to remember to appreciate these precious moments
    as we live them.
We walked along the oceanside this morning.
For a fleeting moment,
there were perfect, tiny footprints ahead of me in the sand.
Three sets of them.
I noticed their perfection and their beauty before the waves
        covered them.
When the waves receded they were gone
    as if they had never been there at all.
But the imprint of those tiny feet were left in my memory.
As are these priceless moments.

Grandmas
Are For Sharing The Moon

There are times in this very real world when there just isn't anymore to say: you've analyzed and dissected and talked and questioned yourself right through to a dead-end street. Times when you've done and said all you can and searched your soul and you have to just leave a matter with the Lord. Bill and I were at just such a place in dealing with a particular problem. We had so saturated our lives with it that it had even filled the crevices of our home, and we had to get away for an hour or so with the children just to collect our souls.

They were bathed and in their pajamas, so we scooped them up, got into the car and went for a quiet moon-lit drive. Except for the gentle summer night noises of the crickets and the kissing of the tires on the damp pavement, there wasn't a word, not a sound, and there was relief and healing in the silence.

The babies were sleepy; we were lost in our thoughts. Suzanne and Benjy were staring intently out of the window.

Softly and dreamily from the back seat—

"Benjy?"

"What?"

"See that moon up there?"

"Moon."

"Don't you wish we had a big airplane?"

"Airplane."

"If we had a big airplane, we could go right up there to the moon and break off a piece of it."

"Moon. Big Airplane."

"Benjy, know what I'd do with a piece of the moon?"

"Moon."

"I'd bring it home and show it to grandma. That's what!"

"Gammaw! Moon."

At that moment I was overwhelmingly lonesome, echoed voices of a little girl running through golden fields of grain and jumping from a hay mow, bulging with the pungent harvest flooded my memory. And I longed to once again run up the old steps of the field-stone porch where grandma would be sitting and pour out the longings and pain of my heart. Grandma who always understood and dried the tears. Irrational grandma who thought her grandkids were extra-smart, extra-beautiful, extra-

special, and extra-right. Grandma who never thought it was silly, never cared about the mess, always believed in the impossible and ever shared the dream.

Even now, living in a very real world with very real problems where my own objective evaluation of myself says irrevocably that I just don't always measure up, that there is much I cannot do, that there are more talents and abilities I lack than I possess, I still need at least one person who thinks I do, knows I can. A grandma is like that, and I guess that's why we need them so. Parents are, of necessity, practical. They *must* discipline, must be realistic, for they are responsible for how their children "turn out." Oh, but grandmas! Grandmas are for sharing a piece of the moon!

I shall live in the practical world of a mother and deal with the nitty-gritty—perhaps until the day when I shall be once more transformed by the trusting eyes of a child into someone who can see all things, understand all things, believe all things, hope all things, and endure all things. For someday I, too, shall be a "grandma" and shall once again be free to share the moon!

Raw Material

There it all lay—
      the boards, the sacks of nails
          the cement mixer, the black stacks of roofing
          shingles.
    There were A-braces and concrete blocks,
          sand piles and bags of dry cement.
Someday, I thought, it will all take shape.
    It will be beautiful and cozy and warm.
Some of these days all that will be
      walls that ring with laughter,
          a kitchen filled with the sweet smells of suppertime.
    There will be a fireside with popcorn and games.
    There will be special private places someone will call
    "my room"
          where a boy can work out chords on his guitar
          where someone's sister will listen to sad records
            with her hair rolled in orange juice cans.
Some of that over there may someday be a nursery
    where the sweet smell of Johnson's baby powder
      will give way on anxious nights
          to the pungent odor of Vick's vapor
          and quiet lullabies will be traded in for worried
          sighs.
Someday, that will house a work bench
      with hammers, grease guns, a chain saw.
    Or maybe there will be turntables and tape decks
          and tuning forks.
Someday, I thought, that confused collection will be a home . . .
Just then I drove into our drive and saw her
    bobbing down across the yard to meet me,
an untamed mess of joy, sorrow, energy, charm, tears, mud,
          blond curls and skinned knees.
    "Hi, Mom!" she yelled. "Been waitin' for ya!"
Someday . . . I thought . . .

It was almost bed-time
and we were huddled around the kitchen table
having our chocolate pudding
when Amy began slowly waving her free hand through the air,
back and forth, back and around.

"Mother,
can you believe that there's all that air out there?
All over the world,
all around
there's just all that air!
Can you believe it?
Nothing but air all over the world!
Feel it!
Nothing but air!"

More Than Air

It was Suzanne who quietly slipped up behind me
and put her arms around my·neck.
"No, Amy," she said softly,
very wise nine year old big sister that she is,
"There's more than just air . . . there's love out there, Amy.
And you can feel it.
There's lots of love out there."

Benjy looked up with his mouth full of chocolate pudding.
"It's a good party we're havin',
isn't it Mom?"

And I could feel it.
There was lots of love out there.

The Game

The wagon was hooked to the garden tractor, loaded with all sorts of good things for a birthday picnic: hot dogs and fixin's, watermelon, corn on the cob, vegetable salad, fresh garden green beans simmered all morning with a ham bone, fresh fruit and raspberry cake. Amy was jumping up and down with "birthday girl" excitement, anxious to be lifted up onto the wagon, while Suzanne and the cousins were perching themselves on every possible corner of the tractor.

I started on down the hillside to the creek with a pot of hot coffee while Bill brought the tractor, supplies, and children

around through the garden gate. Benjy and Grandma had gone on ahead and as I reached the bottom of the hill, I could see them under the willow tree playing with a little plastic ball and bat. Just as I got in ear-shot, I heard Benjy's disappointed little voice cry out, "Grandma, you missed again! You missed my bat again!"

We laughed at the time about his two-year-old immaturity—the way he had it all backwards, this game. The way he slashed away at the air with his little plastic bat, blaming the ball and the pitcher for his misses!

We went on with the party chuckling to ourselves. There was lots of fun and games and eating and boat rides and running—and for Benjy, lots of fighting with almost everyone before the day was through. When we were roasting hot dogs, he wanted to roast marshmallows; when we were running races, he wanted to go for boat rides. At the end of the party, with all the playing and running and fighting, Benjy was exhausted. He held his little arms up at me and begged, "Carry me, Mommy."

I carried him up the hillside to the house, and he went to sleep on my shoulder before I got to the top. I took him up to his little room and laid him on his green bedspread, and stood there for a moment looking at him sound asleep, his blond hair all pasted to his forehead, catsup on his nose, a dirty little baseball still clutched in his hand. I bent down and took the baseball from his hand, and as I held it, looking at that tiny boy, I saw in him a lot of the struggles I had had, trying to grow up as a Christian—times when I had acted like a spiritual two-year-old, standing with my own neat little set of needs and longings and desires in my hand, saying in my more subtle way to my family, my husband, the church, the world, and everyone around me, "You missed again! Here I am with my needs all ready to be met, and You missed again!"

And I was tired that day, the kind of tired that comes from struggles on the inside, struggles that no one knows about but you. Struggles that come when the Lordship of your life is not really clear. So I knelt there that day beside that sleeping little boy, and I gave it all up—the conflicts, the struggle, the doubts—and I asked Jesus to come in as really Lord of all, Lord of our home and marriage, Lord of our finances, Lord of the future and the past, Lord of my failures—really Lord of *all*. Then the struggle ceased and the contentment came, and I wondered why I hadn't done it long ago.

Perspective

I have a little shadow
That goes in and out with me
And what can be the use of her . . .

On second thought, I have no trouble at all telling you the use of her. She helps me make cookies and fold clothes and carry laundry upstairs; she delivers things to the neighbors, answers the phone, and fetches the dog's dish from wherever it is he always seems to take it. Lots of helpful little things she does, this little shadow of mine.

It had been one of her especially helpful days ("I'm weally helpful awen't I, Mommy!") when her big sister came home tired from school and gave her several more little chores to do. Amy did them all, too, but by this time she was getting tired herself and not at all sure that this old deal of being three and "mommy's little helper" was quite all it's cracked up to be.

About this time Daddy came in from the office, tired and preoccupied with the day's problems and asked her to go out and get the paper for him. It was the last straw! She was suddenly fed up to *here* with being helpful, and I saw it coming! She stopped, wheeled around on her heel and started to tell Daddy she wasn't about to do *one more* thing! Then she saw his face and the weary angle of his shoulders. She stopped, just looking at him.

"Oh, Daddy!" she finally said, "I can't say 'no' to *you*!"
Lord, there are times when I just feel "put upon"
   by those who would give me one more thing,
      "just this once."
It seems I am always getting more involved than I intend to
   in the hurts and jobs,
         caring too deeply,
           carrying too much,
              taking on something (or more often
                someone)
            that seems to need a little extra
              and there is no one else to give it to who
                really cares.
And mostly I love it.
   I love people and work and involvement,
        but sometimes it seems I'm carrying the whole load
          and other people are "getting off easy."
And then I see Your face
  and Your load
  and Your love for me
  and I realize all over again
  the price You paid
      for the joy and beauty
    that has made up such a big part of my life
        since I met You.
Well, I just can't say "no" to You, Lord.
  Thanks.

No Looking Back

It was before dawn that the children and I climbed into the car. It was to be a very short visit so we wanted to leave early and pack all we could into the day. Bill was too tied up with work to get away, so we were going alone. I noticed that Amy (only three) kissed him and hugged his neck a little tighter than usual, but it wasn't until we were turning onto the interstate that I learned why.

"Mommy," she asked softly. "We're coming back, aren't we? We are coming back?"

"Day after tomorrow," I answered.

It was ten minutes farther down the road.

"But Mommy, he won't be lonesome will he? I left him my best doll, so he won't be lonesome will he?"

I kept thinking of the little family fragments that had slipped away in the pre-dawn darkness, never to return.

"Bless the beasts and the children, for in this world they have no voice . . ."

Rainbows Live At Easter

Amy—"Sunshine" I call her—is an almost always cheerful, a see-the-best-in-everything child, whose face looks like one of those "Have a Happy Day" signs with the corners of her mouth always turned up in a grin. As you might guess, her favorite color is "lellow" (as she calls it), and she has a "lellow" room with "lellow" curtains and bedspread and "lellow" slippers and a closet with as many "lellow" dresses as we will let her buy.

It was a rainy stay indoors day that she was working in her room with some Playdough—"lellow" Playdough this was. Soon she came bounding down the stairs to the kitchen where I was working, and holding her chubby little hand up to me she bubbled, "Look, Mommy, what I made!" I looked and there on the palm of her hand was something that resembled a hot dog bent in the middle. She chirped on, "It's a rainbow, Mommy! It lives at Easter! Did you know that rainbows live at Easter, Mommy?"

Long after she went back to her room and her work, the Rainbow stayed. How good God had been to us. How very rich we had been, I thought, as I remembered back across the days we had shared:

—*racing down the hillside to the creek to check the mother Mallards for a brood*

—*sitting on the porch in the dark listening to the crickets and the spring peepers*

—*listening to bedtime prayers like the night we all had colds and the house reeked with germs when Amy prayed ". . . and God, please don't let Jesus get a cold."*

—*watching the children race to "play tent" with daddy under the dining room table, with their survival kits of peanut butter sandwiches and milk (Bill's idea of roughing it!)*

—*the fires in the winter*

—*the warm early mornings in the summer that we pulled our little red wagon, loaded with frosted flakes and milk, through the dewy grass in search of a good breakfast spot.*

Special things, simple things. Things that are beautiful and good because of the dimensions Jesus brought to our lives.

Then I thought of the times I had heard folks say,

—Just wait 'til my ship comes in . . .

—If fate would deal me a good hand . . .

—If the wheel of fortune would ever stop on my number . . .

—Someday, when I find the end of the rainbow . . .

But life is not a series of chances; it's a series of choices. Yes, Amy, "Rainbows live at Easter", and life begins with Son-rise, and beautiful things come only from the Lord Jesus.

Since Him, it has been Easter all life long, rainbows and all.

To Be A Man

The little fellow was playing on the floor with his trucks that fine spring morning. His Grandma was standing at the sink washing a dishpanful of tender fresh leaf lettuce, one of the first to be harvested in town.

"What are you going to be when you grow up?" the Grandmother asked the child.

The boy crawled across the floor pushing his toy tractor, making motor noises with his mouth.

"Would you like working in a big factory or having an office of your own? Are you going to be a teacher or maybe a fireman or policeman?"

The child crawled closer to the back screen door open to the pungent fragrance of freshly-turned soil. He ran his little tractor up the door, then stopped, looking out at his grandfather, plowing the warm earth with the garden tractor.

"Nope," he finally said, "I just wanna be a Man. Like my grandpa!"

**Lord,
our world is so in need of heroes.
Give us fewer "professionals"
and more men who stand tall
in integrity and gentle-strength and godliness.
Thank you that a real one lives at our house.
Amen.**

Children

Children.
The fruit
of the seeds
of all your finest hopes.

Value

You came and you took.
You took time
and energy
   and time
and attention
   and time
and love
   and time
and elbow grease
   and time
and my sleep
   and time.
But you brought more.
   You brought sunshine
      and bubbles
    and music
   and laughter
    and sandboxes
    and playdough
  and yellow ribbons
and flesh-colored bandaids
    and arpeggio scales
   and "The Waltons"
    and roller skates
and blow-up kites
    and
    joy.
You were the best investment I ever made.

Tomorrow

"Oh, Daddy! I can't wait! Just think! Tomorrow we go to Florida. Oh, Daddy, I'm so excited! How many more hours 'til we leave?" He was jumping up and down, clapping his little hands, bugging everyone all day long and just counting the minutes. Finally his daddy said, "Hey, why are you so excited? You've been to Florida before!"

"I know, Daddy," he sang out. "But I've never been TO-MORROW!"

There's a song that says, "I believe in yesterday," and I guess a lot of folks could call that their theme song. Our furniture stores are loaded with artificial artifacts of another day—

—pots and kettles and coffee grinders,
—fireplace bellows and rocking chairs,
—pseudo-antique furniture and dishes,
—pretend churns and lard pots.

Anything that was a part of yesterday when life was simple and "home" meant "love"; when people took time to really see each other and "family" included grandparents, aunts and uncles, and all manner of shirt-tail relations. Most of us believe in yesterday because the memories were ready-made. Because it was someone else's world and we weren't responsible for it. And while we sing the nostalgic praises of yesterday, today slips through our fingers leaving us frantic collectors of the symbols of yesterday, conning ourselves into believing that somehow acquiring the trappings will bring the tranquility.

But give me a child—the eternal optimist—who will greet everything life has to offer, even routine schedules and could-be failure with the happy outlook of "but I've never done it tomorrow!"

Today's experiences are tomorrow's memories, and all the artifacts in the world will not make our children remember what it was really like to churn butter, and build fires, and bake bread and play with their daddy in the snow, or pull taffee or ride into the sunrise on a bicycle as a family with breakfast in a brown paper sack.

Memories, important yesterdays were once todays. This is one of them someone may have walked this way before, but we've never gone TOMORROW!

PART 2

Rainbows In The Mainstream

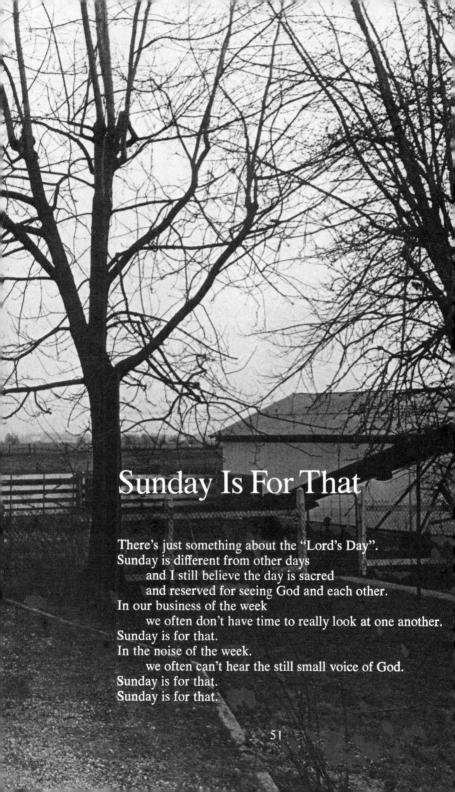

Sunday Is For That

There's just something about the "Lord's Day".
Sunday is different from other days
  and I still believe the day is sacred
  and reserved for seeing God and each other.
In our business of the week
  we often don't have time to really look at one another.
Sunday is for that.
In the noise of the week.
  we often can't hear the still small voice of God.
Sunday is for that.
Sunday is for that.

Reinforcement

Before the eyes of a helpless child,
A little bird winged once again
    Its way to azure skies.

The child gazed long at the struggling bird
That seemed to n'er its task disdain,
    A wish, her only word.

But as she stood with thought intent
On what the creature stood to gain
    And what his courage meant,

The tiny bird his struggling ceased,
And there before the child's wide eyes
    An eagle strong was he.

Courage, once imprisoned long
By failure's cruel and heartless guise
    Was leased and soaring high.

The girl with wonder learned the gist
Of vict'ry from this creature wise—
    'Tis strength with patience kissed.

Still eyes afixed 'pon bird and blue,
She too felt strength with which to rise,
    Her silent wish come true!

Wish I Could

Children, God.
So thankful that you made one.
Wish I could have stayed one . . .

This Day

There is beauty in the morning
    With the sun tip-toeing in,
When the day's a brand new conscience
    And the world's a chance to win.

There is muscle in the noontime
    When the sun is plowing through
Hot and bright and clear and brawny,
    Nature's time to go and do.

There's a charm about the evening—
    Gentle, loving like a friend,
Smiling o'er the west horizon,
    Tying up the day's loose ends.

Lovely, complicated wrappings
    Sheath the gift of one-day-more;
Breathless, I untie the package—
    Never lived *this* day before!

A Regular Day

Thank God for regular days.
There are far too few of them.
With morning chores,
noontime lunches,
naptime stories,
picking up children from school,
fixing supper
to the accompaniment of imperfect piano practice in one room
and Sesame Street in another.
After supper we all took a bike ride,
sang a song,
and finished folding the clothes.
Then we all played on the swing set
and shot a few baskets.
All that couldn't be bad stewardship of time once in awhile.

Home

Home.
A place where
when you get
there,
you know your
heart has been
there
all along.

This House

I love this house!
And nothing gives me more pleasure
          than sparkling tile
               and the fresh smell of Spic 'n Span and Lysol
. . . unless it might be
          the laughter of happy children
               filling the spaces in between
                    the freshly scrubbed walls.
It seems so simple
          appreciating life for what it is
               pleasure and pain
                    joy and sorrow.
For the moment,
     for today, at least
          I can say in all things
               I have learned
                    to be content.

"Until A Year
From June Do Us Part…"

How do you dress to go to a divorce?
  She was half giggling when she said it.
  A tear dropped simultaneously on the plain
  brass button of her plain grey suit.
  He called to see if she had a way.
  She did.
  So they met on the courthouse step
  and walked together to the Directory of Offices.
  An old lady next to me watched them.

Look. I'll bet they're gettin' married. I just love weddings don't you
  They came to the end of the hall where
  the double-pronged arrow pointed both
  directions, paused, then turned to the left,
  where once not very long before they had turned right.
  They knew where they were going.
  The way was clearly marked.

  On the bench outside they sat together
  and chatted amiably about how to properly
  and pleasantly dissect a life.
God must wonder sometimes if this whole principle
of the free will is a good idea.

The Tiny Soap That Grew

The parsonage was just across the street from the school-house, so it was a rare occasion indeed when I got to take my lunch in a real lunch bucket and stay all day at school. A church convention of some kind took my parents out of town so arrangements were made for Grandpa to drive into town in his even then antique car and pick me up when school was out.

I'll never forget the lunches Mother used to pack. Thick meat sandwiches with tomato and lettuce, a red juicy apple, homemade cake, and a slice of longhorn cheese, and always a surprise at the bottom of the lunch pail—a stick of Juicy Fruit Gum, a package of lifesavers, or a nickel for some penny candy from the gas station across from the school. The envious kids who were *used* to taking their lunches would always stand in a semi-circle around my desk to watch the unveiling of the noon-time delicacies. Invariably I would trade the nutritious meat sandwich for peanut butter and jelly and the homemade chocolate cake for a Hostess *Twinkie.*

After lunch we would play soft ball, climb trees, or roller skate on the sidewalk. Since the Creator did not see fit to endow me with a high degree of co-ordination, I was always the last one chosen when the ball teams were divided up, the one stuck up in the tree when the bell rang, and the one with side-walk burns and skinned elbows when the skate keys were put away. On mild days in spring and fall we spent our free time building "huts." These were made by weaving sticks in and out of the fence at the corner of the school yard, laying boards and branches across the corner for a roof and then tightly patching all the crevices with leaves, mud, and grass. We made dishes

66

and utensils out of broken grass and pieces of tin from the trash barrel and furniture from stumps, racks, and orange crates that had been discarded in a gaping hole behind the school. This is what we were doing the day I ran back into the building to get something to use in the hut and happened by Mark Henry's desk.

I always stood in awe of the Henry boys. They were well-dressed, mannerly, and definitely in control. No one picked on them! They were self-assured, with little tolerance for "girls and sissies." I liked them but always felt awkward and suddenly aware of scuffed shoes, disheveled hair or a torn hem when in their presence. Well, this day I came skipping by Henry's desk and my eyes fell on a tiny box of Ivory soap, still in its wrapper, the kind that comes from motels. I had never stayed in a motel in my life and I was suddenly overwhelmed with the desire to have that miniature symbol of adventureland. The room was empty except for me, so I slipped my hand into his desk, took the tiny treasure, walked to my desk and quickly put it in my empty lunch pail. I turned quickly from the room and ran back to the hut and went on as if nothing had happened. No one knew.

No little third grade girl ever spent a more miserable afternoon. The joy of the independence in "staying all day" was gone. The time that usually sped by so quickly crept by at an agonizing snail's pace. The lunch bucket that carried the stolen booty seemed to be larger than life. I watched Mark Henry for the painful moment when he'd notice the soap was missing and report it to the teacher. But he didn't notice, and I was alone in my misery.

Finally the four o'clock bell rang and I walked the long path to the old car where grandpa was waiting. Today I didn't bound up on the running board. The ride to the country had lost its beauty and the farm I loved so much held no excitement for me. I couldn't think of anything to do with myself, though usually there was so much that there wasn't time for it all.

At least I knew grandma wouldn't find me out. She didn't think I ever did anything wrong. Today I was also thankful that she was nearly blind because I knew she could not find the guilt in my eyes. But somehow she sensed something was wrong, and asked if I was sick. "No," I mumbled, "Just tired," as I walked in to lie down on the couch.

"Here I'll just clear out the papers and wash out your lunch pail." I stopped. Paralyzed. "What's this? What a cute little soap! Where'd you get it?"

"I found it, Grandma."

She never questioned my word. She just cleaned the lunch pail, put the soap back in, and went on about her work.

I wanted to die. I had never lied to her in my life. I had never stolen anything in my life. Her total trust and belief in me was far worse than any punishment. I had betrayed someone who loved me, and one sin had led to another. I had no idea that taking a cute-little soap from Mark Henry's desk would lead me to lie and betray the confidence of one of the dearest people in my life. All I could think of was a verse from my junior class, "Be sure your sin will find you out. . . ."

It was a painful five hours before Mother and Daddy came to pick me up on that Friday night. The next morning Mother opened my lunch pail, found the soap, and, like she always did, knew my mind and heart. "Where'd this come from, Gloria?" She always came right to the point. No use lying to her. "I stole it from Mark Henry's desk." She gave me one of those serious talks, picked up one of the handy little pieces of lath that was always around when Daddy was remodeling the old parsonage, turned me over her bed and warmed my backside with it for what seemed like a very long time. Along with the sting that only a lath can give, I felt a great relief that finally I wasn't alone in my misery.

When the spanking was over, she said, "On Monday, you must take the soap back, give it to Mark Henry and tell him you're sorry." Then began two more very long days of thinking about the moment I would stand before the dreaded Mark Henry and tell him I had stolen his soap.

By the time I actually walked up to Mark on Monday and face to face apologized, I had vowed with all my soul to *never* get into a mess like that again. As it turned out, motels and bars of soap were old stuff to him and he couldn't have cared less. The insignificance of a material possession and how the thirst for it could distort its true value taught me eternally the meaning of the afore obscure word "covetousness."

The whole ordeal was a *heavy* price to pay, to learn the very valuable lesson that "the way of the transgressor is hard." But far worse **than** the actual act of stealing for me and the punishment of that wrong, was the pain that lingers with me to this day that I took from my precious grandmother who loved me, a trust and confidence that did not belong to me and that I had not earned.

Life's School

Long ago in someone's musty classroom
such terms as "the human condition"
         and "man's existential dilemma"
used to fly by my brain like dried milkweed seeds
in the summer breeze.

Occasionally I'd catch one
take it apart
and try to understand it.
But for the most part they remained little entities
                    unto themselves,
removed from me,
detached from any total concept
        that had any relationship to living.
I memorized long boring definitions,
became accustomed to the feel of the verbage spilling
                from my lips,
and wrote acceptable answers
    on white paper with blue veins running through it.

But I never put my finger to the real pulse of mankind.

Today I saw a dirty child riding on some mother's hip.
Tired and hungry and mute.
A tiny child
    a child with could-be's.

The child moved her little bird-like hands
      around the woman's neck
to get a better grasp on life
and listened with innocent acceptance
      as the woman loudly cursed
      the out of order sign on the phone booth.

Today I saw my husband turn to the man behind him
      in the check-out line of the discount store
to ask him whether the steak house down the street
      was open yet.
The blank expression behind the tired eyes told me
      that behind the "I don't know"
was the regret that life had not offered him such luxuries.
Luxuries like first hand knowledge.

Today the taxi-cab driver went to sleep at the wheel
      and crashed into the rear end of a brand new station wagon.
The despair in his oath
    Oh, I knew things were going too good
carried overtones of a hand-to-mouth existence
      I'd never known.

I'd like to take that class again.
I think this time
      I'd catch a few of those seeds
called the "human dilemma."

71

Compassion

In the midst of all the throng at Disneyland
I saw a tiny flower wilt and nearly die.
I walked on by.
It was so small it hardly caught my eye.
A bag of popcorn later,
the hot sun made me stop to rest beside the tiny plant again and
    lo—
A better Samaritan than I had beat me there and left behind
Four tiny icecubes and a bit of diluted coke.
It wasn't much, but to the tiny flower it had been "Life".
I hope I'll not walk on by any more chances to give "a cup of cold
    water".
Or whatever.

The Real Thing

Since Suzanne was the only child in our family for four years, she invented three playmates: Baffy, Mellow, and Guillicutty. Now, Baffy began as a baby boy who she would carry from place to place or lie gently on the rug or grass while she played. (I remember a terrible fit of crying she had one day when I unknowingly sat on the chair in which she had laid Baffy.) Baffy grew. He was her charge. She taught him to talk and walk and play.

Then there was Mellow, a little girl just Suzanne's age—an equal and devoted friend with whom she played games, talked on the play telephone, and shared. And there was Guillicutty. Guillicutty was evidently a grown-up of neuter gender—a *confidant* who listened with patience and sympathy to the many grievances a child can have growing up in a houseful of parents. Guillicutty was one adult who really understood.

And so the three of them, imaginary though they were, became very real to us all. Suzanne even occasionally demanded that I set places for one or the other at the dinner table.

Then came the day when we learned that a baby was on the way, a real one. We gently broke the news to Suzanne, who responded immediately with, "Great! It will be Baffy!" Without comment on her suggested name, we began to plan. We chose paint for the nursery, bought some new things and got out the little things Suzanne had worn. We even bought mother-daughter dresses for Suzanne and me to be saved and worn on the day when we would bring the baby home. A couple of times I tried to talk to Suzanne about the possibility that the baby might be a girl and that we ought to pick out a girl's name. "Nope." She would always dismiss the suggestion. "It will be Baffy!"

The morning after Amy was born I called Suzanne on the phone. "You have a precious little sister," I told her. "She is beautiful with a round chubby face, sky-blue eyes, and lots of black hair. We have named her "Amy" and you will just love her." After a long silence, she asked if she could hold her on the way home. "You sure can! and bring my dress like the one you have so I can wear it home with you."

She wore her dress, and my little look-alike held the baby all the way home. She became my indispensible right-hand-man and she loved Amy with great devotion. With all the visits from our countless relatives and with the new schedule of formula, diapers, sleepless nights, and baby business that Amy had put us on, it was almost two months before I realized that I hadn't heard anything about Baffy or Mellow or Guillicutty. And I haven't to this day. There was just something about real live, functioning, tangible Amy that made the other three unnecessary, and like Puff the Magic Dragon, they were relegated to the immaturities of the Past.

Learning to share in the "very Being of God" is like that.

"The Word, God's personal expression of himself to me, became a human being and lived hereon earth among us and was full of loving forgiveness and truth, and we have seen his glory—the glory of the only Son of the heavenly Father."

And that's for real.

PART 3

Rainbows And Love

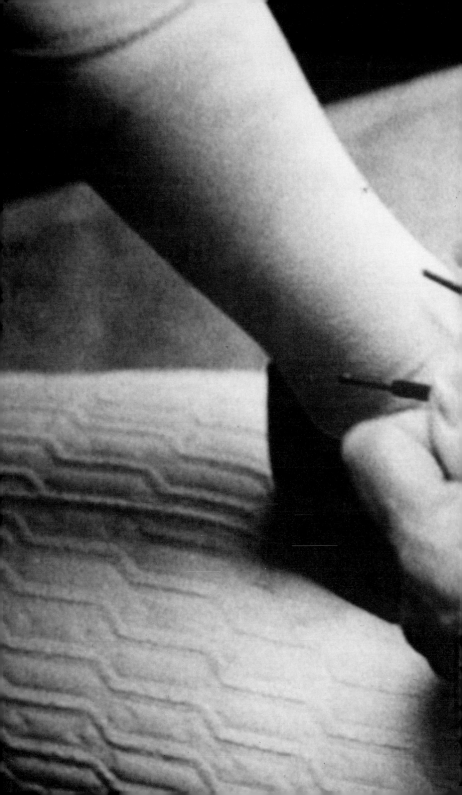

Eden

It was all so beautiful in the beginning.
Everywhere she looked
        the Garden stretched out in all directions,
                perfect and lovely
                   and free.
There were fruits of every description—
        flowers that dazzled the eye with their glorious color.
And the animals!
        Gentle, unafraid and beautiful—
           some strong and huge,
              some tiny and weak.
                But all lived together there
                   sharing the loveliness of the Garden.
The morning sparkled in the dew.
        The freshness of it almost took her breath
           as Eve woke in a bed of blossoms
                and stretched her long slender arms.
She sat up and looked around her.
        The fragrance of the flowers begged her to pick them.
Before she knew it, she found herself
    skipping like a child across the hillside
        gathering blossoms and braiding them as she went
           into a lovely garland.
        The colors of it rivaled only
           by the perfect, flawless blush on her own cheeks.
God was near,
        Life was beautiful
           and her heart was full!
There was Eden in today.
    And the beauty of it
        almost made me forget the chapters Life has written
           since the first one.

The Fighter

"Well, you can't win 'em all,"
he said with a shrug of his shoulder that day
when the last of his dream finally crumbled away.
And he managed a bit of a lopsided grin
that gave me a hint of the greatness in him.
"I may as well quit!"
But I knew by the glint in his eye
he'd go straight as a dye to the scene of defeat
and he'd try one more time.
It was part of his nature to try and try
so tho' his lips said, "I'm through,"
I knew what he'd do.
"You can't win 'em all . . ."

"But you can,"
said the soul of his being,
"win some."
And he won!

Il Fait Froid, Mon Coeur

As the barren twigs shiver
 under the sullen blasts of winter's frozen breath,
  so my heart pauses
   paralyzed by the thought of losing you.
 Or worse—
  having you to hear and see
   but having lost your love.
Marriage must of necessity be,
 the union, not only of two bodies,
  but of two spirits, two souls
   with hopes and dreams unique to the world
    but twined each to each.

What would there be worse than to live in a house with one
 whose face was not the mirror of happiness and delight,
  but instead a screen to censor deep emotion
   from one who lived to see it pictured there?

What worse than to have the kisses of love's confession
 turned to chill reminders of a lie?
What worse than to have the uniting of two bodies
 no longer be the outward symbol
  of the inward unity of two souls.
 To change one eagerly submitting to her love's embrace
  into a mere physical receptacle for lust's release.
 Or to see those strong masculine arms
  trade love's bidding for duty's call.

And worst of all, to see love vanish in the little ways.
 To see no more the flicker of nocturnal candlelight
  dancing with the shadows to some secret lover's tune.
 To feel no longer a gentle touch, a warm caress.
 To lose forever the right
  to discard one's plans to please another,
   the joy in sharing,
    the delight in knowing
     that you belong.

The final chilling stroke would end it all,
 to care no more and never stir again.

Friendship

It's to my friend that I may speak my mind,
    knowing that he will not revel in the flaws
        he sees there.
I need never be afraid
        to bare my soul before him,
But he would not for morbid entertainment
    uplift the cover and intrude the sanctity
            of my heart.
I know my friend is always there
            (a comforting thought)
But the depth of our friendship is not measured
    in numbered rendez-vous.

Our hearts are close,
    a nearness that transcends proximity of human form,
For thoughts, like mountain nymphs, dance
        from the dewdrops in the meadows of my mind
            to those of his. Those meadows
    need not run to meet each other, and yet
They are all one: the meadows,
                    the dewdrops,
                        and the nymphs.
My friend can bear to watch
                as burning tears
            burst from my eyes;
He does not fear to fix my compass
        when I have veered off course,
                or to remind me
It's not a broken compass
                but that I have forgotten
            that North is North.
Yet he does not live to say to me "You're wrong!"

We are as two great painters, working in the same room.
We share at times our paints
        so that each may achieve a perfect color,
But we are creating separate masterpieces.

Worth The Risk

Love is but a game, some say,
     yet I would say
It is no game at all,
     it is not "play".
For games are made in part
     of "Let's pretend"
And love that's worthy of the name
     has not a trace of pretense.
I would rather call it art.
Never has there been a masterpiece
     that did not express the very essence
     of the artist's soul.
When a painting goes on display
     in a gallery
    so do the inmost secrets
     of its creator's being.
Yet, that is the price one must pay
     to be an artist.
That is the cost a painter sits to count
     before he lifts the brush.
But if he dares to pay the price
     and commit his soul to canvas
He'll not go unrewarded.
     If he is true and expresses well,
Time and oils join to work a miracle
     that grows yet richer year by year.
And so it is with love.
     There is no love at all unless
One dares to give his very soul to it.
     He cannot save some corner in reserve
To salve the fear of being scorned or trampled,
     but must give all as would an innocent child—
an innocent child—freely and without guile.
Such love expressed is masterpiece enough
     whether so acclaimed or not.
And if it finds acceptance and adoration,
     that is a bonus that will grow
Deeper, richer as the moments pass.

Upward Mobility

How far above in worth and fame
You are than I.
My spirit's light is but a faint flicker in the darkness
beside the stately waxen strength of your fine beam.

You call me equal
how true to your humility,
and yet I seem a mere basker in your sun,
a flower open to Nature's nectar,
or at a race, the observer of the run.

You asked if I could love you.
"Yes," said I,
but what injustice was that answer to my heart's true cry.
For were I to choose one boon to ask of life,
one pleasant pasttime indulged me along the way,
T'would be the right to breathe, "I love you" every day.

Until I See You

The fading sun has left its pink and amber traces on the horizon
     just where the sky touches the silvery ripples of the lake.
The duty outline of one lone sail can be seen in the distance.
A gentle breeze is just strong enough to move
     the heavy black-green mantle of the giant oak above,
But still gentle enough to blow teasingly through my hair.

No longer are happy summers splashing playfully at the water's
     edge.
The lake plays another role at evening time.

Now and then I catch a glimpse of lovers strolling hand in hand
    whispering the things I long so much to hear tonight.
How many days in my life have passed without my noticing.
How different have been these days
                                without you.
I'm learning how long twenty-fours can be.
I've learned to remain silent when I'm bursting
                                to express myself.
I've gleaned your letters as Ruth did the fields of Boaz
    waiting for that moment when I too can say
                                "Whither thou goest . . ."
The blinking lights across the water reminds me of the world
                                of reality.

Time enough for dreaming.
Until I can dream with you.

To Sing Is The Thing

There are some things a heart can't say
There has to be another way
To let it out or die that day!
    And so I sing.

Sometimes a soul's too full to speak
Of beauty so it has to seek
Expression in some manner meek—
    And so I sing.

And when the heart is broke and sore
And I can't stand it anymore
(I'd really like to rage and roar!)
    Then I just sing.

Then there are days packed full of joy
Like when they say, "Ma'am, it's a boy";
When tiny hands grasp their first toy,
    I have to sing.

When everything I am responds
To lover's chant and touches fond;
When I would forge sweet friendship's bonds,
    I choose to sing.

I've learned the things are very few
We civilized have left to do
To let folks see inside of you,
    Except to sing!

Ode To Autumn

O autumn, thou hast robbed me
Of my senses,
Drained from me life and breath.
With all thy beauty!
I should have stopped my ears
When first I heard thee
Calling gently through the frosty air.
But, O, how sweetly
Beckoned me, thy siren's song.
One note—my ears were thine.

My eyes I should have blinded
When first I glimpsed
A petal etched in tawny brown.
But wide-eyed as a child
I watched, as you began your promenade
Down forest trails,
And at your touch I saw the world transformed
To festivals of color
And saw the leaves begin to fall
Like wine and citron nectar drops
To fragrant pools below.

By this I could not turn my eyes away;
I could not stop my ears
Nor seal my senses from your pungent scent,
But then and there dismissed my will
And yielded
To your sweet embrace.

I Like Being Married To You

I like being married to you . . .
    I like the way you put on your sox
        Insist on wearing your rundown, slip-on Hush Puppies
        (when everyone else is wearing tie-up oxfords),
        Refuse to throw away your old wine-colored pants
        just because they have a little white paint on the cuff
          Persist in believing in people.
I like being married to a man who thinks everyone should
    plant a tree
        face problems squarely
            spend time with his own children
                quit smoking
                    be himself.
I like being loved by a man
    who will tell you the truth
        say what he means
            make valid evaluations . . .
Because when you hold me close and tell me
    that you love me,
        I feel there must be something good inside me
          after all!